T0031034

Dachshunds

Dachshunds

Jane Eastoe

Illustrations by Meredith Jensen

BATSFORD

First published in the United Kingdom
in 2024 by
Batsford
43 Great Ormond Street
London
WC1N 3HZ

An imprint of B. T. Batsford Holdings Limited

Copyright © B. T. Batsford Ltd 2024
Text © Jane Eastoe 2024
Illustrations © Meredith Jensen 2024

All rights reserved. No part of this publication may be copied, displayed,
extracted, reproduced, utilized, stored in a retrieval system or transmitted
in any form or by any means, electronic, mechanical or otherwise including
but not limited to photocopying, recording, or scanning without the prior
written permission of the publishers.

ISBN: 9781849948401

A CIP catalogue record for this book is available from the British Library.

10 9 8 7 6 5 4 3 2 1

Reproduction by Rival Colour Ltd, UK
Printed by Leo Paper Products, China

This book can be ordered direct from the publisher at
www.batsfordbooks.com, or try your local bookshop.

MIX
Paper | Supporting
responsible forestry
FSC® C020056
FSC
www.fsc.org

Contents

Introduction

Guten tag! I'm a dachshund, fondly dubbed a sausage dog, dixie, dackel or wiener, depending on where you live. Short in stature, but with a giant personality, I'm one of the sweetest, most loving and devoted dogs you could wish for.

Mentions of my breed can be traced back to 15th-century Germany, and though there are theories out there, our origins, and the crossing of breeds that produced the dachshund are uncertain. Our breed was recognized by the Royal Kennel Club when it was founded in 1873, and the American Kennel Club followed suit in 1885. We were popular with Queen Victoria who was introduced to us by her German husband Prince Albert.

From the 1950s onwards we dachshunds have become increasingly popular as a breed, consistently making the top ten rankings. According to the Royal Kennel Club, miniature smooth-haired dachshunds were the fourth most popular pedigree dog breed in 2022, and in the same year the American Kennel Club ranked the dachshund at number nine in the USA.

The name dachshund translates as 'badger dog'. The clue is in the name – the breed was developed to hunt badgers. It's therefore no surprise that we're feisty, determined and independent.

I'm incredibly loyal and loving. We dachshunds like nothing better than curling up on your lap or beside you. I worship the ground you walk on, and hate being separated from you. Most dachshund owners will admit that their dogs sleep in their bedroom, and often on (and indeed in!) their bed.

We are also sensitive, vocal and will bark at anything; other dogs, squirrels, the postman, the neighbours, when we're excited, when we're being protective, when we're left alone, to get your attention. You can train me to understand the 'quiet' command, but I will never be silent. We have selective hearing and are slow to train, so you'll need persistence to get us to do what you want.

I've real character and will amuse you endlessly as I race around the house. I may be small, but I've a lot of energy and no sense of physical danger. I should not climb up things, or jump down from heights, but I will. Dachshund owners frequently get ramps to enable their dogs to nestle beside them on the sofa so they can access this nirvana without needing to jump.

I'm playful, and you'll have to be constantly on your guard. I will chew anything and everything I can get my teeth into – an electric flex is irresistible, but toys are favourite amusements. Mealtimes are my favourite time of the day. I'm greedy, which helps with training, but don't overindulge me as I'm inclined to obesity.

Dachshunds can make good family pets given the right circumstances. We are best introduced to children as puppies, otherwise we will view them with grave suspicion. We may look like a soft toy, but we will not enjoy being treated like one. Children must not pick us up and carry us around. Nor must they chase us, drag us out of our beds or get in the way at mealtimes. Because we're small, we can be easily frightened and get defensive, and then we might be inclined to snap or nip. If you see us shaking, cowering or baring or teeth near children, this means that we're struggling. Children must be taught to treat us with respect and we in turn will learn to respect and love them.

Digging is my great passion, and I'll dig with enthusiasm throughout my life. I'll dig up your lawn and sniff out anything that a squirrel has buried and eat it. I will dig up your bulbs to see if they are tasty – be careful what you plant around me, as some bulbs such as daffodils and hyacinths, are poisonous to all dogs. I've a keen nose and will seek out and find ANYTHING that smells interesting to eat, without thinking about the consequences. It doesn't help that dachshunds have a delicate stomach and are prone to gastric upsets, so you need to be on the alert in the garden and when you take me out and about.

Digging aside, I'm a clean dog, though my low-slung silhouette means that I get splattered with dirt and my tummy gets wet. I don't like the rain; coats help but you may find I simply refuse to go out – fortunately I'm portable.

Our distinctive characteristics include a deep chest, long muscular body, short legs and a long whippy tail. The breed was refined for hunting purposes to produce a dog that used its nose to scent and track, combined with a robust physique that enabled it to enter burrows to flush out prey. We were originally much larger and heavier than today's standard dachshunds. Miniature dachshunds were bred to chase after smaller prey such as rabbits and hares.

Further selective breeding, believed to be with spaniels, produced a dachshund with a long coat, suitable for colder climates; these long-haired varieties tend to be a little gentler and more relaxed. Breeding with terriers produced the wire-haired variety, that could cope with thorny undergrowth, and which is lively and loud.

While we're the sweetest companions who hate to be separated from you, don't mistake us for a lap dog. At heart we're hounds – albeit small ones! We are lively, determined hunting dogs who won't think twice about taking off after prey. We don't need long hours of exercise and are happy in a small house or a flat with a little garden. But we're most definitely a DOG, and as long as you understand that we will get along fine. Once a dachshund owner, always a dachshund owner!

Jip

Owned by Tom & Denise | Lives in Rotterdam, The Netherlands | @dachshund_jip

Jip is a sweet, social and funny rabbit
dachshund. When she's not asking for playtime
or cuddles, she's looking out of the window on
neighbourhood watch.

Puppies

Dachshund puppies are bundles of energy that have two speeds: GO and out for the count. Remember we push to get our way, so you'll need to take control right from the start. Our owners can be inclined to baby and spoil us, but we need to be treated as dogs! I understand all too well that I'm hard to resist, but it's essential that you kindly and gently teach me how to behave right from the start.

When you come to meet us for the first time you'll be questioned carefully by our breeder as to what you want from us. Do you want a show dog or a pet? What kind of a pet do you want, loving or lively? According to your answers you may only be shown a couple of puppies to choose from that best suit your requirements.

You should meet my mother and possibly some of my other relatives too. My father might not be around to see as he may live some distance away, but you should see a picture of him at least.

A litter of dachshund puppies is adorable, but speaking dachshund to human, let me give you some words of wisdom: even if you plan to have two dogs eventually, don't get them from the same litter at the same time, no matter

how great the temptation. Dachshund puppies are a handful – we're playful, strong, boisterous, we chew anything and everything and need masses of attention. If you take me and one of my siblings, we will become reliant on each other and pay you little heed. What's more, as we mature, we may fight to determine which is the dominant dog in the pack. A pair of female dachshunds are likely to get territorial, which can cause no end of problems. So if you want two sausage dogs, start first with one and only get a second when the first is well trained. The first dog will lead the way with all the basic training techniques.

Home Preparation

Once a sale has been agreed you should make a few preparations.

Arrange to take a good chunk of time off work to help your puppy settle in. The more secure I feel from the start, the better your chance of limiting my separation anxiety. If you can't take much time off work, you'll need to arrange for someone else to be with me.

I'm an escape artist! As a small puppy I can, and will, wriggle through tiny holes or gaps. Check that your garden has adequate fencing, and repair as required or plug small holes with logs or chicken wire.

You'll probably find that a big adult bed may overwhelm me at first, so initially it's good to have one with soft sides so that I'm protected from draughts, and this will also stop me slipping off in my sleep. Soft cloth doughnut beds with tall sides and a cushion inside will help to keep me calm, and make sure there are blankets for me to burrow under. Dachshunds sleep a lot, and the message is 'Do not disturb' when I'm sleeping!

Get me a crate, not to keep me in, but to give me a safe bolthole. I will appreciate it if you cover this over with a blanket to stop draughts, put my bed in it and a heated pad to simulate the warmth of my siblings. If you put paper or a puppy pad on the floor of the crate I can relieve myself in the night. I won't usually soil my bed, but accidents happen and when small I will need to pee during the night. Please check my bedding in the morning to make sure it's dry, and wash it if it's wet – we like to have clean bedding. You should also purchase a supply of poo bags – compostable bags are available.

You can shut the door at night, after I've been out for a pee. Then you can sleep easy in the knowledge that I can't run around in the night. In the daytime, it should not be used as a cage, although you can shut me in for short periods if you are going out.

Leave both a food and a water bowl for me the whole time. Stainless steel is durable and easy to keep clean.

I LOVE, LOVE, LOVE toys. If I start to nibble or nip your fingers, you can give me a toy to chew on instead – my teeth are like needles! I will get the message that one is acceptable, and the other is not (see the training chapter for more advice). Soft toys are particular favourites, though they will get destroyed, and harder toys are helpful for teething.

You may want to get me a lightweight puppy harness and a lead, even though you won't be able to take me out for a walk for a few weeks. It's not safe for me to mix with other dogs, or to be anywhere that other dogs have been, until my vaccinations kick in. However, it's important to take me out and about for socialization. Carry me around and you'll be mobbed like a film star because I'm so cute, but bear in mind that attention can be overwhelming.

Stair Gate

Containing your puppy initially can be useful. Restrict them to a room with hard flooring so that accidents can easily be cleaned up. If you live in a house with stairs a stair gate is a must, as climbing and jumping is particularly harmful when we're young. I also feel safer in small, confined spaces.

Things to hide out of sight:

- Shoes, socks
- Electric wires, plugs and cables, mobile phones, TV remote controls
- Children's toys
- Medicine or chocolate in your handbag or briefcase, or lying around
- Slug pellets, mouse traps and garden chemicals
- Cleaning products – plastic bottles are tempting to chew
- Your underwear – highly embarrassing if I turn up with a pair of your pants in my mouth, plus I may eat them!

House Rules

It's a good idea to agree house rules in advance of my arrival. Am I going to have the run of the house, or only be allowed in certain rooms under supervision? Am I going to be allowed on the sofa or the beds? If so, you'll need ramps that enable me to climb up and down safely. Can you live with this?

Please scour the house in advance for things that could be harmful. I cannot be trusted to be sensible, possibly for the next two to three years!

Training Basics

Training starts from day one, but before you leap to that chapter, make sure that everyone in your household is familiar with the basics. Agree as a household what specific training words you'll use in advance; I will grasp clear one-word instructions much faster. Use *sit* – not 'sit down', *down* – not 'lie down', *wait* if you want me to stay in one place until summoned, *stay* – if you want me to remain put until you return to me, and *leave* if you want me to let go of something. I will also need a trigger word for going to the toilet (read on).

House Training

Brace yourself, we dachshunds are notoriously hard to toilet train. Start collecting newspapers or buy puppy pads in preparation. It's much harder to house train dogs during winter when the doors are most likely closed. Umbrellas or covered areas can help sausage dog puppies to avoid the dreaded rain.

Don't leave me in the garden alone when I do the deed. I like to be with you so will only worry about where you've gone and not focus on weeing or pooing. When I'm a puppy, I will probably want to pee every time I wake up from a sleep and pee and or poo straight after every meal, so take me outside every two hours as a minimum – hourly is even better. Each toilet break I'm making scents that will trigger a similar response next time. Try to stay outside with me for a bit after I've done my business, play and let us have some fun – you are rewarding me for being good.

Agree on a key word you'll use for toilet training that you don't use frequently – my owner uses 'bumbles'! Use the agreed word when I'm peeing or pooing, say it over and over again quietly and gently. Avoid saying I'm a 'good girl/boy' as this may become my trigger phrase to urinate.

In time I'll learn that when you use this trigger word you want me to wee or poo. If everyone does this, I will learn much faster. Make a HUGE fuss of me

Dachshund Fact

- E B White, author of *Charlotte's Web* and *Stuart Little*, and enthusiastic dachshund owner wrote about the experience of training his dachshund Fred: 'I would rather train a striped zebra to balance an Indian club than induce a dachshund to heed my slightest command. When I address Fred I never have to raise either my voice or my hopes. He even disobeys me when I instruct him in something he wants to do.'

every time I do it outdoors – I need to understand that you are happy when I do this!

Make a mental note of where I like to pee outside and take me to that area when you want me to use the facilities. Some dogs like a dry surface such as gravel, stone or concrete, others only wee on short grass – we all have our preferences.

At night I can last for about four to five hours without weeing. Some owners set an alarm to take their puppy out. Others keep one ear open and whisk us outside if they hear us wriggling, depending on where we're sleeping. I'll gradually be able to manage for longer at night.

If I do have an accident, don't shout at me – it will only make me nervous and frightened, or make me hide away. Say 'NO' firmly if you catch me in the act and carry me gently into the garden, then praise me effusively when I wee.

Clean up the accident area with an enzymatic cleaning material – biological washing powder mixed with warm water in a 1:9 ratio will remove smells. If you don't do this I will always be tempted to return to the same spot. Household disinfectants should be avoided as they contain ammonia, and the smell of this may encourage me to soil the same area again.

The Journey Home

We sausage dog puppies usually leave our families between eight and 16 weeks old. Extra weeks spent with our siblings can help our socialization and confidence and lessen our anxiety so it's worth the wait to ensure we're more secure. By this time I will be weaned, but be prepared, I may come with a list of dietary requirements for the first few months and my breeder should give you some of the kibble I've been eating to help me settle in with you. This should help avoid tummy upsets. Vomiting or diarrhoea can dehydrate a puppy quickly. Please follow the breeder's guidance.

I will also have been microchipped, wormed and may have had my first vaccination. My breeder will give you my Kennel Club documents that have full details of my lineage.

When we're small we're easy to pick up, but you must be extremely careful how you scoop me up. Use two hands, one under my chest and one under my rump because my long back is easily damaged and must be supported.

The journey to my new home may be trying. Remember, I probably won't ever have been in a car, and I may cry for my siblings. I may pee, poo or be car sick, or I might just fall asleep on your lap. It's a good idea to have some old towels and some kitchen roll to hand, or even a change of clothes!

Car-sick dachshund pups grow out of it, so don't let us develop a phobia about the car. Keep putting us in it, stay with us and give us treats – we don't need to go anywhere. Then take me on a short journey so I learn that being in the car is not a scary experience.

When we arrive home for the first time put me down in the garden to give me a chance to relieve pent up tensions – remember to stay with me!

Welcome

When you bring me into the house put me down and let me sniff around for a little while. Please don't overwhelm me with attention, especially if there are children in the house. Let me go to them and sniff them, and take things at my own pace, as it will be a scary experience for me. Then show me my bed, some toys and where my water bowl can be found. After a little time, give me something to eat, then take me outside straight away for a toilet break.

First Night (start as you mean to go on)

Given the choice I will sleep with you, in your bed. I will be sad and lonely without my siblings and without you. I will cry. If you can't cope with this, keep me close for a few nights until I've settled in. Some people tuck the puppy bed or crate beside theirs for a few days, so that they can reach down and stroke us for reassurance. I will get used to sleeping by myself in time. A small, cosy bed with sides also means I can rest my back against it as I did with my siblings.

Most sausage dogs I know wind up sleeping in their owners' bedrooms, even if they start off by sleeping elsewhere!

Healthy Eating

Dachshund puppies have four small meals a day once they are weaned. My breeder should give you a sample menu and some of the packet food I've been eating to avoid any tummy upsets from dietary changes. Don't change things until I'm settled and happy in my new home, and do so gradually, incorporating the new food little by little.

Sausage dogs are naturally greedy, so I will usually gobble up every last morsel. If I don't eat, keep an eye on me as I may be unwell. Lift my food bowl up after ten minutes and don't offer me food until my next mealtime. If I'm still not eating after 24 hours, you may need to get me checked out by the vet.

By 12 weeks I can drop to three meals a day, and at six months I will be ready for two meals a day. I will be fully grown from around nine to 12 months – at this stage I can go onto adult food.

Recall

Start working on this as soon as you have settled on my name. Have treats to hand. Call my name in a slightly higher pitched voice than usual and sound excited. When I come to you, reward me with a treat and make a HUGE fuss of me. Let me go then repeat. If I don't come to you try running away from me and call me – reward me when I come and make it a fun game! Stick to my name only – no other words, like 'here' or 'come'.

Treats

Keep treats strictly for training purposes – don't give me anything off your plate, as much as I gaze at you with my big round eyes. This will be hard because as I grow, I will become an expert in emotional blackmail. Try to remain firm, as once you have fed me from your plate, I will thereafter expect a taste of everything.

The Vet

Most vets like you to register with them as soon as you get a puppy. They will give me a once-over to weigh me, test my microchip, get my vaccination schedules in place and discuss flea and tick treatments. They will also make a fuss of me so that my first visit to the vet is a positive experience.

Charlie & Luna

Owned by Susanna | Live in London, UK | @charlie.sausagedog

Short and sassy, cute and classy. Breaking hearts
in South London since 2018.

Vets will probably know about puppy socialization classes in the area and usually have lists of useful contacts for the future such as kennels and dog sitters.

> ## The following vaccinations are required in most countries:
>
> - Canine parvovirus
> - Canine distemper
> - Hepatitis
> - Leptospirosis

The vaccination schedule varies slightly from country to country so be guided by your vet. Some diseases require me to have an annual booster to ensure continued protection. The vet will advise you and will normally send out a reminder. All these diseases are extremely unpleasant and are easily passed on. Please make sure I'm vaccinated as a puppy and that you maintain my annual booster jab schedule to keep me safe.

Keep your vaccination certificates secure. The vet can update them as required and you'll have to show them if you need to put me into kennels. No reputable kennels can take an unvaccinated dog.

A rabies vaccination is required in some countries and will be required if you intend to travel internationally with me. This is not a quick process; rabies vaccinations need time to become effective and I have to have blood tests to ensure I have sufficient immunity. Allow an absolute minimum of six to eight months for this process. You'll also need to ensure that I have my annual rabies boosters.

Harness or Collars?

While I'm in quarantine and have to be carried about, take the opportunity to get me used to both collar/harness and a lead. Be forewarned, I will not enjoy this experience. Start with the collar/harness; put it on for a few minutes, give me treats, then take it off. Make sure that you can slip two fingers underneath a collar or harness and remember to check the fit regularly.

Once I've had a few days to get used to the harness try me with the lead. A few minutes at a time for both. Lots of treats please!

There's considerable debate as to whether a collar or a harness is better for the dachshunds' long frame. There are pros and cons to both. You are advised not to use choke collars on us, but by the same token, my collar must not be so loose that I can easily slip out of it. Harnesses can stop us from pulling, without choking us, but they can rub, especially if we get wet from being so low to the ground. Some research suggests that harnesses can increase our chances of developing spinal problems, but there's no conclusive evidence yet.

Walking

I love to race around the garden and the house. Let me do this as much as I like because I have the choice to stop and rest whenever it suits me. Puppies under three months don't need walks; their vaccinations haven't usually taken effect until this time. Once our vaccinations have kicked in start walking me for five minutes a day, building up to a maximum of 60 minutes over the course of the day, two 30-minute walks daily is ideal. Some dachshunds enjoy more exercise, but generally we aren't built for long marches or accompanying you on a jog.

Social Niceties

Sausage dogs especially benefit from puppy socialization as soon as their vaccination schedule permits. We love our own people but can suffer from anxiety with strangers. Be gentle with us – you might need to sit and watch the class with us until we look sufficiently interested in the proceedings. Submissive weeing is common when we're little – it's our way of showing that we know our place, so outside socializing might be a good idea.

When puppies mingle, expect a lot of butt sniffing! For some reason you humans seem to find this ritual impolite, but it's simply our natural way of saying hello, so please don't tell us off. It also teaches us to recognize the signals that another dog might not be so friendly – if a dog stands with a stiff body and tail, with its hackles rising and ears back, I have to learn to back off.

We can be wary of bigger dogs. If this is a problem, try to introduce us to dogs that are friendly and gentle to boost our confidence – work from middle-sized upwards.

Puppy socialization classes usually include some element of group training and help teach you how to get me to focus. The instructors will also teach you dog training techniques. Frankly, these classes are as much for you as they are for me. You have to learn how to handle me effectively so I will behave beautifully for you. You might think I'll never learn how to do anything, but the dog trainer will show you, with terrifying ease, how easy it is to get me to do what you want.

Don't blame me if I behave badly. It's all down to you – keep on with my training every day and wait to see how smart I am. Remember, there are no bad dogs, just bad owners. Don't forget to take poo bags and high-status treats with you whenever you go out. Treats help to keep me focused on you and what you want me to do.

Nervous Puppies

Most dachshund puppies are bold, but others suffer from anxiety. It's important that you take me around a range of situations: busy roads, stations, cafés and parks so that I can meet different men, women, children, dogs of all breeds and get used to the strange noises around me. I need to see all sorts – bicycles and wheelchairs, people

in hats or carrying walking sticks; every experience will help me adjust to the wider world. Don't wait to do so – carry me if my vaccinations haven't kicked in.

If I'm nervous of other dogs when I'm old enough to go out and about, don't scoop me up. This will only reinforce the notion that I'm top dog and that I'm in grave danger. Talk to other dog owners and ask if it's OK to stroke their pets and chat to them, but don't push me forward. Let me see you being open and friendly and let me build my confidence at my own pace.

Separation Anxiety

All dogs are pack animals and are happiest when they have you, the pack leader, in their sights. Dachshunds are incredibly attached to our family and hate being left behind on our own, especially when young. You may have to arrange for me to spend part of the day with a relative or friend or put me into doggy day care so that I've plenty of company, exercise and entertainment.

Try not to reinforce nervous behaviour from the start. If your puppy hates being away from you, encourage them to play then leave the room for a moment – keep playing and popping back so they get more confident that you'll return.

The same applies to teaching me to get used to being home alone. Only leave me alone for a few minutes initially so I don't get the chance to panic. Tire me out before you leave so that hopefully I'll fall asleep, then build up the time you leave me little by little.

Give me a fantastic toy to play with, such as one filled with treats, so that I'm kept busy and occupied and am not stressed because you aren't in sight. A Kong can be useful – you can fill the inside with meat and freeze it so that I have to work to release the tasty filling.

Dog charities recommend that no breeds are left alone for more than four hours at a stretch, and this is certainly as much as we can cope with. Moreover, our bladders are small and we will need to relieve ourselves.

Digging

Because we dachshunds consider digging to be something of an art form, we may try to bury our toys to keep them safe. If this is a problem, try to distract me with something more interesting when I start. Alternatively, allow me to have one place where I'm allowed to dig and take me to this spot if I start digging elsewhere. Try a sand pit, and bury my toys there for me to find.

Travelling Companions

If you take your sausage dog puppy on trains, buses and the underground when they are small they may be fearful at first, but they will get used to it and behave calmly. Car travel, though you might not think it, has more restrictions.

In the UK, the Highway Code states that dogs and other animals must be suitably restrained. The interpretation of this is loose, however for your sake and mine, please ensure that proper restraints are in place.

The most effective way to keep me safe is to have a crate in the rear of your car, fitted with a bed, to minimize the distance I can be flung in a crash. If you accustom me to the crate at home, I will be perfectly content to travel in this. Dog harnesses that clip on to seat belts can be utilized in a back seat if this isn't an option – if in the front seat an air bag going off could seriously harm your dog. I should not travel on your lap.

Hormones and Bitches

As I move towards my first birthday the hormones will already have kicked in; in developmental terms a one-year-old sausage dog is the equivalent of a 15-year-old human, though theoretically they are fully mature by this age!

Dachshund Fact

- In the 1939 film *The Wizard of Oz* a miniature dachshund called Otto, owned by Margaret Hamilton who played the Wicked Witch of the West, had been cast as Toto, Dorothy's devoted sidekick. Due to anti-German feeling with the outbreak of the Second World War, Otto was replaced by a Cairn Terrier called Terry. L Frank Baum, the author of the book, never specified what breed of dog Toto was.

Most female dachshunds will have their first season (proestrus) between the ages of six to 18 months and then every seven to ten months thereafter. Don't consider breeding a litter of puppies – dachshunds don't reproduce easily and it requires the specialist expertise of a breeder to bring a healthy litter safely into the world.

Your bitch will be on heat for around 21 to 28 days. She may well become cranky and for good reason: her vulva will swell, her nipples may swell, she'll bleed spots of blood and she'll also need to urinate more frequently. There are a number of ways to deal with this, but please bear in mind that as well as being cranky, she'll also be clingy and want to be with you – isolating her in a room with hard flooring will make her miserable if she is used to being with you.

Nowadays, you can purchase pants for bitches on heat. She can wear these in the house, but she may take great exception to this addition to her wardrobe. You can cover her bedding and the sofa with towels and wash them regularly, and you can cover

carpeted areas of the floor with towels or newspaper. You can clean spots as they appear and then have your carpet professionally cleaned when she has finished her season. Try not to let any irritation show – she'll pick up on this.

Keep her in close contact when she is on heat; male dogs will find her irresistible and they can pick up her pheromone-filled scent from a long way away. Only let her off lead when you can do so safely or choose to walk her at times when there are fewer dogs around.

If you also have a complete male dog in the house, your life is about to get difficult. One option is to persuade a friend to look after your male dog until your bitch has finished her season, or alternatively you can keep your dogs apart. The use of stair gates or crates can allow the two dogs to still see each other, but not to interact.

Some bitches get uncomfortable when they are on heat, and a trip to the vet may be required. The vulva can become painfully swollen and her constant cleaning can aggravate this problem. If her nipples become distended, she may be producing milk and will require medication to stop production.

Neutering your bitch once she has had her first season will give her protection against some forms of cancer and infection of the uterus (pyometra). Speak to your vet about the best time to have her spayed. She doesn't need a litter of puppies to be happy, and because this breed has health implications it's best left to specialist breeders.

Hormones and Male Dogs

Most male dachshunds are fertile before they are fully grown, somewhere between six and 12 months of age. Speak to your vet about the best age to have your dog neutered.

Males sometimes act before we think, as the testosterone is surging! In fact, for a short while, young male dogs have more testosterone than adult dogs and this can lead to a sudden outbreak of territorial behaviour. Scent marking territory is an early indication of sexual maturity – when your male sausage dog continually stops for short wees to signal where he has been. You may also find to your horror that a perfectly house-trained dog suddenly lets you down by peeing inside a friend's house, a shop or a pub. This can happen with all breeds. Own up to their offence and offer to clean up the puddle.

Perfectly amiable sausage dogs can suddenly start having stand-offs with other dogs. Don't panic, this doesn't necessarily mean your sweet boy is going to become an aggressive monster. Male dogs have to deal with a whole new set of signals from other males, who may suddenly be aggressive with them. Your puppy needs to learn to revaluate the social signals he is getting. He will learn.

When dealing with some aggression for the first time, you'll need to exercise your dog well and increase training; reinforcing good behaviour will help.

If you are struggling, seek help from a professional dog trainer.

Training

Because I'm smart and stubborn, you need to be patient when training me, and assume the position of top dog, the leader whose rules I follow. If you don't, I will try to usurp you and assume the pack leader position, despite my diminutive size! Please don't allow this to happen because I'm a terrible decision-maker, and if I feel like I'm in charge I may get increasingly anxious and protective.

Don't indulge me. It's harder to break established bad habits, such as barking, if you let me get away with it for the first year of life.

I'm close to the ground and my sense of smell is extremely good, so I can easily be distracted by interesting odours. Because I love playing, if I'm not having fun in a training session I may simply try to divert your attention, and I don't have a long attention span, so make sure to keep sessions short and end with a game to reward my efforts.

The fact that I'm food-motivated is a plus, but use high-status treats – i.e., not any old dog biscuits – to encourage me to do what you want. Consistency and kindness in training right from the start will enable you to overcome any issues in time. You'll need to wean me off

As a starter, be aware of the basic rules we must both adhere to:

- It's your job to keep me under effective control. You must have a lead with you every time we go out and use it when necessary to keep me safe on the roads, when signage requests it – often when nesting birds are in the vicinity – or around livestock. Never let me roam unsupervised.
- Don't let me approach cyclists, runners or other dog owners unless invited. Always put me on the lead if you see a horse and rider.
- Don't let me race off lead across private land or through crops – though this isn't usually a problem with dachshunds as we like to stay close to you, but nevertheless be aware.

- Never let me worry or chase livestock.
- Be safe around livestock. Check fields before entering so you aren't caught unawares.

Keep a good distance from livestock and give them plenty of space. Cattle and horses can be curious of dogs and protective if they have calves or foals. If livestock comes worryingly close release me so that I can get away and you can too.

- Always bag up my dog poo and take it with you – this can be disposed of in special dog poo bins or, if none are around, any public litter bin.
- Don't leave bags of poo on the path to pick up later or hang them from branches of trees. It's too easy to forget them or lose them. Pick up as you go.
- Put an identification tag on my collar with your contact details on it. Put your name on it (not my name) and a phone number. Remember to update this and my microchip details if we move home.
- Keep my vaccination and worming treatments up to date.

treat-based training in time, as I can gain too much weight, but it's a useful tool to begin with.

If I'm not properly socialized, I may view all runners, cyclists and small children with grave suspicion and try to nip them at every given opportunity. I may decide that trains and buses, or certain noisy places are simply not safe and refuse to enter. If I'm nervous I can become aggressive, so be patient with me, use treats and show me that you are taking me somewhere safe. My confidence will gradually increase and any tendency to nervous aggression will decrease.

Training me is the key to keeping me under control. The more you train, the better behaved I will become, but it's a long process.

Dog Training

Attending puppy socialization classes and dog training classes will help us both to develop a good relationship and will help you to teach me good manners and how to behave. Please remember that I don't speak your language; you'll have to patiently teach me how to do what you want. I won't understand the words, but I will learn what you want me to do when you make certain sounds. Learning appropriate hand signals will help me to further understand what you want. Training dogs is not difficult, but it requires time and patience from you. Two short, five-minute sessions daily will help me learn. If you put in the time I will repay you (most of the time anyway) by behaving beautifully.

Initially you can train us using treats alone, but you can graduate to clicker training as you progress. Clickers are used as a training tool to mark good behaviour. This is a small device that you hold in the palm of your hand which emits a click when pressed – an audible pat if you like. When we hear the click we know we have done something good and that we will get a treat. It's an effective reward system that flags up good behaviour. The use of the clicker can be expanded to promote and encourage new and developing good behaviours every time you spot them. Don't point the hand holding the clicker at us, keep it by your side.

Nora

Owned by Alysia | Lives in the USA | @lifewithweenies

Nora is always up for a grand adventure and belly
rubs. She loves treats and snuggling up on the
couch whenever she can.

Start by putting a treat in your closed hand and hold the clicker in your other hand. I will focus on your hand as I smell the treat. When I do this, click the clicker and at the same time, bend down and open your hand so I can access the treat. It's imperative that you get the timing of the clicks right – you only want to use it to reward good behaviour and it can take a bit of practice to master the technique efficiently. In time, you may be able to use the clicker alone as a reward, but this will take time and effort.

Basic Commands

Keep training sessions short and please don't bother me with training if I've just had a meal or if I'm tired, as all I will be interested in is sleeping. If I've just woken up and am dashing around the garden, you might find it hard to keep me focused. Pick the moment when I'm likely to be at my most receptive.

Recall

This is the first lesson and a basic piece of obedience: you call, I come running. Some of us learn to come to our names quickly and easily, others are rather more wilful. I may have short legs, but I can reach speeds of between 15 and 20 miles per hour! It's only in quick bursts, so it's important I come when called.

Call my name and sound excited. Use 'come', not 'come here', or 'here'! When I respond, reward me with a treat and make a HUGE fuss of me. I'll learn quickly. Once I've grasped this you may want me to come to you and sit, before I'm rewarded (see opposite).

Even when you think we have mastered this technique, we will let you down on occasion, and as teenagers (around six to eight months old) we can become stroppy and develop selective hearing, like humans!

If this happens reinforce your original technique with lots of repetition. Call me back repeatedly and reward me with high-status treats. You don't have to make me sit to get a treat, instead hold the treat in a clenched fist and make me touch your hand with my nose, then release the treat. Use the words 'off you go' to tell me I can go away and play again. Repeat and repeat at random times throughout the walk.

If you only do this at the end of the walk, I will learn that it's not a good idea to come back to you. It's best to get me on the lead before the end of the walk when I just think I'm returning for another treat. Try to keep one step ahead of me mentally.

Lavish praise upon me every time I come back to you. As I become more reliable, you'll notice that I keep looking back to check where you are. This is a good sign; it indicates that I'm attuned to you, that you are important to me and that I want to keep an eye on you to ensure you don't suddenly disappear.

A whistle can be useful. It will save you from having to bellow my name. Plus, a whistle expresses no emotion, so I won't pick up on any anger in your voice if you are getting frustrated.

If I'm proving resistant to recall, try not feeding me before a walk and keep those high-status treats to hand on the walk. This helps to reinforce the message that you are the source of all good things and that coming to you brings real benefits.

Sit

Put a treat in your hand and close it into a fist. Hold your hand over my nose and say 'sit'. Lift your hand slightly upwards and backwards – as I lift my nose up to follow the treat I will naturally drop my bottom and go into a sit. Praise me.

Once I've grasped this command, practise saying it with me beside you as well as in front of you.

Get me to sit before you give me my meals. As I become more disciplined you can make me wait to go to it until you give me the 'off you go' command.

Down

Start this training once I've begun to grasp the 'sit' command. For good results at the start, do this training where I can lie down comfortably, either on my bed or on a rug.

Get me to 'sit' and reward me. Put another treat in the palm of your hand, say 'down'. Then move your hand slowly towards the ground, edging it just out of reach as my nose follows your hand down. I will lower my front legs and with a bit of luck my hindquarters will follow. If I get up to try to reach the treat, pop

me back in the sit position, give me a treat, then try 'down' again. It might take a few attempts before I figure out what you want me to do, but I will get there.

Once I'm beginning to grasp this instruction, you might like to introduce a hand signal to support it. With the treat in the palm of your hand extend your index finger and point it downwards. Take the treat to my nose and repeat the same process with your hand so that I lie down. Make a huge fuss of me every time I get this right.

When I've grasped the basic principle, start practising the command away from my bed – I'm well upholstered and will happily lie down on command virtually anywhere.

Wait

The wait command teaches me to stay where I am until you tell me what to do next. I'll wait until you put my food bowl on the floor and not get under your feet in my effort to get at the food. I'll wait at gates and doors while you go ahead of me.

To teach me 'wait' first tell me to 'sit', then take a step backwards, still facing me, holding your hand palm up, then call me to you. You'll probably have to do a lot of practice before I start waiting. Keep up with short bursts of training and I'll get the message. Keep distances small and gradually extend them as I'm following the instruction reliably. It doesn't matter if I lie down instead of sitting, so long as I stay put. In time you'll be able to leave me sitting waiting while you walk a distance away, and there I will remain until you call me.

Use 'wait' every time you feed me. Make me sit, then tell me to wait until my food bowl is on the floor. I will keep getting up and try to rush it, but just raise the bowl in the air, put me back in the sit position and tell me to 'wait' again. If you do this at each mealtime, it's an easy way of reinforcing the command.

Stay

'Stay' training starts in a similar way to 'wait'. Put me in the sit position, take a step forward with your right foot, holding your hand behind you with the palm facing me. I will probably get up and follow. Put me back in the sit

position and try again. Eventually you'll be able to take a step forward and then step back beside me without my moving.

Praise me effusively when I do as you have asked. Try to walk off with your right foot leading for the stay command, this is a visual clue for me. It's difficult but important, as it sends me a clear signal that I'm doing a stay exercise (you set off with your left foot instead when I'm walking to heel).

Extend the 'stay' distance a little at a time. Keep repeating the word 'stay' slowly, clearly and firmly. Turn and face me before you return to me. As I get even better at obeying you, when you have gone as far away from me as you wish, turn, face me and wait for five seconds before returning. Keep extending the time you wait at a distance – ten seconds, 30 seconds and so on.

In time you'll be able to leave me and return to me, walking around the rear of me as I remain in the downward position, where I watch you closely. Praise me calmly and quietly while I'm still in the in the sit position.

Then release me with the 'off you go' command. If I am happier doing this exercise in the down position that is fine too.

Heel

Though I'm small, you move slower than I like when we're out on a walk, as there are things I want to see and smell and I will pull to get to them, though this is less of a problem with miniature breeds. I will be panting and choking in frustration as I attempt to go where I want, at the speed I want.

You need me to learn to walk comfortably beside you, with a slack lead, until you can safely let me off the lead and I can wander where I will. The sooner you can do this the better, so start my training in your garden before I'm even allowed outside for a walk.

Decide which side you want me to 'heel' to and stick to it. In competitive obedience training I should be on your left, and because I respond to visual clues you should lead off with your left foot first to reinforce the message that we're walking to heel. Remember, you lead with your *right* foot when we're doing a stay exercise. You are trying to keep my nose to the side of your leg. This may be too much of a challenge for me to begin with, but with lovely smelling treats in your hand I should remain happily by your side.

Put high-status treats in your pocket and then, using your left hand, grab a few treats and hold them in your fist. Let your hand hang by your side so that I can smell the treats, say 'heel'. I will watch your hand to keep an eye on the treat. At regular intervals, bend down and give me a treat to keep me encouraged. Keep repeating the word 'heel' over and over again while I'm following your instruction. You can also train me to 'heel' in the garden off lead, but remember to have those treats to hand.

If I'm being resistant to walking to heel, another technique you can employ is to keep changing direction without warning. This will throw me as I'm expecting you to keep moving forwards. Every time I start pulling, change direction again. It doesn't make for the most productive walk in terms of distance (and you might feel a little

silly), but it will reinforce the notion that although you are slower than me, I cannot rely on you to plod along behind me. You are taking charge.

You can also pop a squeaky toy in your pocket, as you want to keep bringing my attention back to you so that my lead is slack. I LOVE a squeaky toy.

Getting me to walk to heel will be much easier on the way home as I will have had a good run around, although if I'm fed after a walk I may be in a hurry to get home for this treat!

Leave

This command is designed to make me give up something without a fuss. It can be a life-saver (literally) if I've made off with something dangerous such as a bar of chocolate absentmindedly left within my reach, a blister pack of painkillers I've filched from your handbag or a cooked bone that has accidentally fallen from a plate.

Start training me at a young age by gently trying to remove a toy from my mouth. Say 'leave' in a firm but kind voice. If I hang on to the toy don't pull – tug is a fun game in itself. Just produce another toy and make it seem more exciting than the one I'm clutching in my jaw. Say 'leave' again and offer me the new toy. If I drop the old toy, make a fuss of me and give me the new toy. Reinforce this message over, and over and over again.

Quiet and Speak

Dachshunds are barkers, because we were bred as hunters and barking is instinctive. We will use it as an alert system, to get your attention and to say hello. We will bark when someone comes to the door, and at any strange noises. Despite our stature, we're good guard dogs and see it as part of our role to protect those we love.

Teach me both the 'quiet' and 'speak' commands from the start – don't wait for me to grasp one command first.

Don't tackle teaching 'speak' anywhere undesirable – such as in the house where you want your dog to be quiet. Outside is a good place to start. Use a squeaky toy or anything that encourages barking and when I do bark, say 'speak' and give me a treat. The universal signal is to hold your palm up then move your fingers down and your thumb up at the same time – so your hand looks like a mouth opening and closing.

'Quiet' is a good exercise to work at in the house. If I'm barking, get a treat prepared and when I stop the noisy cacophony, say 'quiet' and give me the treat. The hand signal for this is to hold your index finger up against your lips in a 'shhh' sign. This technique positively reinforces good behaviour. Work at it, and in time your sausage dog will understand what you want and will be quiet for a treat. Loud, barky dachshunds can be a nightmare to live with, for both you and your neighbours, so keep going with this exercise right from the start.

If I go into energetic overdrive and bark repeatedly whenever someone comes to the door, shouting or trying to pick me up when you open the door won't help resolve the issue. Don't give me treats to distract me, because this will reward the barking, instead say 'quiet' gently but firmly and make the 'shhh' hand signal. When I stop barking, reward me.

Obviously, this doesn't help when you have someone at the door, so if

Bun

Owned by Tim & Alice | @bun_thesausagedog

Bun is a smaller than usual dachshund but makes up for it with her big personality. We call her the shadow as she follows us everywhere and is the perfect travel companion.

I'm causing mayhem, enlist a friend or neighbour to help with training. Get them to come to the door and make their presence known. When I start barking say 'quiet' and wait until I stop, however long it takes. When I stop, give me a treat. Get your friend to knock or ring again, and repeat. This will take a little time, but I will catch on. Do let your friend/neighbour in after a while and give them some treats as well by way of repayment. If you can repeat this exercise for a couple of weeks, it will make a huge difference. This exercise also works well if I bark at other dogs when I'm walking on the lead. Stop walking, say 'quiet', use the hand signal and when I stop barking reward me. Remember, I only get the reward when I'm quiet.

If I bark at you in the house to get your attention – I'm stubborn and I can keep this up for a while – ignore me! It's annoying, but don't respond until I stop barking, then reward me straight away.

If the neighbours complain that I bark when you are out of the house, you should walk me before you leave to tire me out – for 30 minutes as a minimum – and make sure I have something to entertain me while you are out.

Jumping Up

Crack down on this right from the start. It isn't good for dachshunds to be jumping up on you, others or on the furniture. When I jump up, say 'down' and ignore me until all four paws are back on the floor. Then praise and reward me.

Overcoming Negative Behaviour

My character will determine how easy I am to train. I may have firm views about how things should be done and resist you initially, but persist and together we will get there in the end. Never punish me for bad behaviour, no matter how angry you are, instead reward me when I behave well. Sausage dogs are sensitive to mood and we will be unhappy and frightened if you are angry with us.

Separation Anxiety

This can easily become an issue with dachshunds who are devoted to their favourite people. If I'm wide awake,

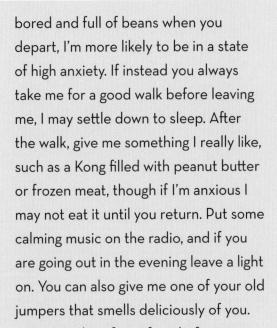

bored and full of beans when you depart, I'm more likely to be in a state of high anxiety. If instead you always take me for a good walk before leaving me, I may settle down to sleep. After the walk, give me something I really like, such as a Kong filled with peanut butter or frozen meat, though if I'm anxious I may not eat it until you return. Put some calming music on the radio, and if you are going out in the evening leave a light on. You can also give me one of your old jumpers that smells deliciously of you.

Don't make a fuss of me before you depart, be calm and quiet, and do the same when you return. I know this is hard because my welcome is so enthusiastic – after all, I love you wildly, and who else is so demonstrably thrilled to see you when you have only been out for five minutes? However, if my behaviour is causing issues this will help me to understand that calm is good, and that your going out and returning is no big deal.

Dogs read human movements, so we will know when you grab your coat, your bag and your keys that you are heading out. If we react badly to this

you can work on us by going through the process of leaving and then returning a few moments later. If you keep doing this we will not get as anxious because we won't be sure you are actually leaving. You want to promote a calm atmosphere. Ignore me when you leave, and for a few minutes when you return.

If the problem is severe, please take me to see a dog trainer, or dog behaviour specialist, as they can help us to achieve a peaceful and happy life together.

Aggression

While the more aggressive characteristics have been bred out, because we sausage dogs were bred as hunters, we can still snarl, nip and bite, especially if we're nervous or feel threatened. If I nip you, even in play, squeal or yelp in pain and leave the room. It will happen, so make sure to respond immediately, as this is a trait to be actively discouraged. A bite on the ankle is every bit as painful as one higher up the body.

As already stated, young male dogs have to get used to other dogs responding to them differently as they grow into adulthood, and you may have a few hiccups. If you suspect hormones are the problem and you don't like the idea of neutering me unnecessarily (thank you for that consideration), vets can chemically castrate a dog, a treatment that is effective for around a year, before you decide whether the snip is the solution!

If I bark and lunge at other dogs, you need to divert my attention to you. When you see another dog coming, get a treat in your hand and distract me with the treat so that I focus on you, instead of obsessing about the advancing pooch. If I've been attacked or bitten by another dog this may also make me more inclined to be suspicious of them. In this case, you'll have to work on my socialization by building up my trust in other dogs and encouraging calm behaviour. Remember, if I see another dog with its hackles up, I'm more likely to respond in kind. Promote calm behaviour.

Ultimately, you are responsible if I bite or attack another dog and you can be fined for not keeping me under proper control. We can be snappy with other dogs, but tend to come off worse in a fight, so work on boosting our socialization and promoting and rewarding calm behaviour. If you are struggling, please seek professional help at the earliest opportunity – your vet is a good place to find contact details for dog behaviourists. If a placid and friendly sausage dog suddenly becomes aggressive, take them to the vet to get checked out, as it may be indicative of an undiagnosed physical problem.

The real secret to dog training is to understand that it's not something you ever stop doing. You can train me to sit and lie down on command, to wait and to stay exactly as instructed, but the one thing you can guarantee, if you don't keep up the training, is that I won't keep behaving beautifully. Keep it up! I'm a lovable, loyal sausage dog – you'll be amazed at what I can learn to do.

Resource Guarding

While dachshunds are loving dogs, if we feel nervous and territorial, we sometimes indulge in resource guarding as a defensive measure. We can get possessive over a particular toy, our food bowl or our bed – wherever that might be.

We might be perfectly sociable outside the home, but hate other people, or other dogs coming into our home. Small children can be a trigger for dachshunds. This behaviour can be startling when it occurs – the dog can stiffen, growl, raise its hackles and threaten to bite. All dogs are susceptible to resource guarding, it's a perfectly natural behaviour in the wild, but less tolerable in a domestic situation. You need to nip this behaviour in the bud but handle the situation carefully.

Your sausage dog is merely trying to protect what he/she regards as a valuable resource, so try to see things from our point of view. If you try to snatch a precious toy away from me, or to take away my food bowl because I'm growling if you come close, I will only guard it more closely next time. Do not get cross, this will only aggravate the situation. You are aiming to diffuse the situation to reinforce positive behaviour and make me feel less threatened.

If I will only allow one person to sit on the sofa with me, get me a new dog bed and keep putting treats in it to make it attractive. Keep me off the sofa. Ideally seek the guidance of an animal behaviourist who can advise you on what techniques to use.

Digging

You may as well face it, digging is in my DNA. I was bred to make my way into burrows, and being able to dig is crucial to this activity. I won't only dig up your lawn, I will try to dig in the house – on rugs, sofas and in my bed. The simplest way around this problem is to give me somewhere I'm allowed to dig in the garden – sand pits are ideal. In the house you'll have to train me not to dig, by distracting me with toys and games. If I'm tired, I'm less likely to want to dig, so make sure you are exercising me sufficiently.

Diet

My strong sense of smell alerts me to the presence of food, and I'm persistent in hunting out its source, whether it's a fragrant free-range rabbit, or something cooking in the kitchen. Obviously, I can't reach the kitchen counter, but I will dog your footsteps and make you the focus of my attention in a bid to get my share. On the plus side, my healthy appetite means that I respond beautifully to food-based training techniques – especially if it means pleasing you at the same time – a double bonus for me.

I treat each meal as a race, even if I'm an only dog. If I'm not solo, I will keep a jealous eye on my fellow dachshunds to make sure I'm getting my fair share of food, and will gobble up my food in seconds, barely tasting it. This isn't good for me. Special food bowls are available from pet shops that make it harder for me to eat quickly. I have to work to access the food in these bowls, using my tongue to tease out every last bit, and this slows down the rate at which I eat. This may have the added benefit of reducing my gassy emissions!

If you are using lots of treats in training, remember to deduct the overall amount from my meal allowance. This way my treats are part of my daily

rations. I'm so eager to please you that once I've grasped the basics, you can try rewarding my good behaviour with methods that won't add inches to my waistline.

We sausage dogs are adept at emotional blackmail. When you are dining, we will plant ourselves beside you and gaze up with pleading eyes. We are willing you, with every fibre of our being, to slip us a morsel of something. If you do, we will love you even more. However, much as I hate to admit it, this isn't a sensible approach. Our propensity to overeat and gain weight means that the simplest and safest approach is to never, ever feed us from your plate. Be firm from the start – the simplest technique is to send me into another room while you are eating.

Being the food provider puts you in a position of great power, so use that power responsibly. Of course, you can ignore my advice and feed me scraps from your plate, but if you do this, you need to give me less food at my mealtimes to counteract these extra calories. Are you prepared to try to work out the precise nutritional impact

Don't give your dachshund any of these foods:

Alcohol isn't much good for humans, and it's not good for sausage dogs either. As well as all the obvious symptoms of alcohol poisoning, sickness and diarrhoea, it can also damage my central nervous system.

Avocado contains persin, a fungicidal toxin that is harmless to humans, but which can cause vomiting and diarrhoea in dogs. It's present in the seed, the fruit, the skin and the leaves.

Caffeine isn't good for dogs. If we consume excessive amounts, it can have a similar effect to chocolate. Don't give us coffee or tea.

Chocolate contains a compound called theobromine, which is fine for humans, who can process it, but it can kill all dogs, even in small amounts. If your dachshund has eaten chocolate call the vet straight away and ask their advice. Note how much chocolate has been consumed and whether it's dark or milk chocolate, as your vet will want to know; dark chocolate contains more theobromine. Depending on how much chocolate has been consumed the vet may want to make your dachshund vomit, and they may administer charcoal to absorb the poison.

Cooked bones are highly dangerous. They can splinter and damage your dachshund's internal organs, often causing perforation of the gut. Raw bones are safe, but only give your sausage dog a large raw bone, as small raw bones can cause choking.

Corn-on-the-cob isn't poisonous to dogs, but it can cause a blockage in a dog's intestine and be potentially fatal.

Grapes, sultanas and raisins can cause liver damage and kidney failure in some dogs. It's impossible to predict whether or not your dachshund might be affected, so don't give us grapes, sultanas or raisins, and please think twice before you offer me a morsel of that delicious carrot cake or fruit cake!

Macadamia nuts are toxic to dogs and can cause severe pain, muscle tremors and limb paralysis.

Onions, garlic and chives, indeed anything from the onion family, are toxic to dogs and can cause serious gastrointestinal irritation and red blood cell damage.

Xylitol is an artificial sweetener used in many low fat and diet products, but it's highly toxic to all dogs, including sausage dogs. It can induce hypoglycaemia, or low blood sugar, and is linked to liver failure and blood clotting disorders.

of those three scraps of chicken and half a roast potato, four crisps and a piece of cheese scone, and deduct the equivalent calories from my dinner? I thought not.

I don't blame you for wanting to feed me from the table, but unless you are extremely disciplined with my overall food intake it's incredibly bad for me. I will gain weight, and this will shorten my life. Sausage dogs are prone to a range of weight-related health issues; indulge me and you could be condemning me to years of ill health and pain. The old adage 'a moment on the lips, a lifetime on the hips', could have been written for a dachshund.

Please don't feed me straight after a walk. Let me rest for half an hour before feeding. This is important, as I can develop a twisted stomach or bloat, which is dangerous. Leave an interval after exercise before feeding me and this problem shouldn't occur.

Weight

An adult standard dachshund should weigh between 7.25–14.5kg (16–32lb), while an adult miniature dachshund should weigh less than 7.25kg (16lb). Our stature is solid and muscular, and our belly should be above our rib cage; if it starts to droop below my ribs I'm carrying too heavy. If I'm only fed at mealtimes and I get one hour of exercise a day, my weight should not become a problem.

A high-fibre, low-fat, complete food diet, with fewer calories per pound, can be utilized to help me shed some weight, if necessary. I won't feel cheated if you feed me this, or you can cut back on portions of my regular food. If you can help get me back into shape I will enjoy exercise more and that will in turn help maintain my proper figure.

All dogs are omnivores, eating both plant and animal matter to survive. However, we cannot eat anything and everything.

Nutrition

There's an enormous array of commercial dog food on the market and, as with human food, there's an increasingly sophisticated wealth of products on offer; wheat intolerance, gluten intolerance, hypo-allergenic,

vegan diets and sensitive tummies are all catered for. You can feed your dachshund a purely dry diet, a mix of wet and dry, cook your own meals, get freshly cooked frozen meals delivered to your door or follow the unfortunately named BARF (Biologically Appropriate Raw Food) diet.

If you study the labels, you'll find it hard to make direct comparisons of the nutrient content between the different forms of dog food. Protein and fat are important components, as are a good balance of vitamins and minerals. Sausage dogs need different quantities of nutrients at different stages of their lives – puppies have a higher protein diet and the requirements of senior dogs (seven-plus years) are different again to that of a lively adult dachshund.

High-quality foods generally contain less fillers and more nutritional ingredients, where cheaper foods will use more fillers to satisfy appetite.

Most adult dog foods contain around 20 to 30 per cent protein (5 to 8 per cent in wet foods) and 9 to 14 per cent fat (2 to 4 per cent in wet foods). Dietary fibre (vegetable matter)

maintains intestinal health and helps to treat both constipation and diarrhoea and has a pro-biotic function. Ash is a measure of the mineral content of food, and includes calcium, copper, iron, magnesium, manganese, phosphorus, potassium, selenium and zinc. There are 13 vitamins that are important for health: vitamin A, vitamin C, vitamin D, vitamin E, vitamin K and eight B vitamins.

Protein usually comes in the form of meat and fish, but vegetables can also supply a cheaper source of protein. Protein from non-meat sources such as soya, maize and potato are harder for the dog to digest and can in some

Dachshund Fact

- **Artist Andy Warhol** immortalized his dachshunds Archie and Amos in his paintings, and David Hockney has done the same with his dachshunds Stanley and Boodgie. Pablo Picasso had a dachshund named Lump.

Neville

Owned by Claudia & Daniel | Lives in Tamworth, UK | @neville.longbottoms

If you're looking for Neville you'll either find him
under a blanket or sunbathing. If he's not there
he'll be barking at the postman!

instances cause dietary intolerance. Raw meat BARF diets have a much higher protein content and, as the meat is uncooked, it retains its nutrients. The nature of the protein content in dog food can vary from pure meat to rendered meat meal, bone or animal derivatives.

Fats and oils are important for a sausage dog's skin and fur, and are also a good source of energy. Some essential fatty acids, such as omega-3, are also important for health, and often added to commercial dog food.

Fillers make up the remaining percentage of dog food. This is likely to include whole grains such as wheat, barley, corn, rice, oats, rye and sorghum, many of which also include important nutrients. It may also include peas, potatoes, sweet potatoes, quinoa and lentils that are higher in calories.

As with all food purchases, you get what you pay for, but your dachshund may well be perfectly happy and thrive with a competitively priced dog food. If you are concerned about quality, don't rely on the front of the packaging for information, look at the ingredients listed on the back. If your dachshund

is thriving, everything is fine, but if they start getting tummy upsets or skin conditions you may have to pay more careful attention to their diet.

Always be guided by your vet. Dogs are less likely to develop food allergies than humans – they have robust digestive systems, but allergies to surroundings are more common irritants. However, anecdotal evidence suggests that sausage dogs may be more prone to food allergies than some other dog breeds; seek professional advice if we're getting skin disorders or runny poo on a regular basis, and don't assume we have a food allergy. Simply changing food brands will do nothing – I will be allergic to an ingredient and not a brand, and you'll need help identifying what the cause might be.

Complete food, a specially formulated diet in the form of kibble, is perhaps the simplest way to ensure that your dachshund gets a nutritionally balanced diet. If it's kept in an air-tight container it has a good shelf life.

Wet food, in the form of tins or pouches, serves up wet meat, and is usually served with biscuits or kibble to ensure all the nutritional requirements are met.

The BARF diet imitates the diet a dog would have in the wild and is high in protein. It consists of 60 to 75 per cent raw meat and bones, which can be in the form of such items as chicken wings and necks, or raw fish. The remaining 25 to 40 per cent consists of fruit and vegetables, offal, eggs or dairy foods and is made up by you to create the nutritional whole. To make life simpler, manufacturers now sell the meaty part of this diet, which is delivered frozen, and portions can then be defrosted as required. You have to be committed to put me on this diet – it's not cheap and requires a lot of proactive food preparation from you. If you choose to feed me the BARF diet, please follow all the usual hygiene precautions in handling raw meat; disinfecting all surfaces that have been in contact with raw meat and washing your hands.

In many countries around the world you can also buy specially prepared, nutritionally appropriate cooked meals online, which are then delivered frozen to your door. This is a premium product. I will love it, but again it doesn't come cheap.

Water

Please make sure I always have water available and wash my water bowl daily. It isn't good for me to drink stale and dirty water – even though I may well drink happily from a muddy puddle out on a walk. Please keep some water in the car for me and a travelling water bowl so that you can always offer me a drink. I often badly need some refreshing water at the end of a walk.

Gourmet Poo

Coprophagia, poo-eating to you and I, isn't a problem for me – you are the one that has the problem with it. All puppies may well try eating poo out of pure curiosity, to see what it tastes like. Bitches lick their puppies' bottoms to encourage urination and defecation, and when the business is done, they eat everything up to keep the nest clean – this is a natural instinct. Some dogs only eat poo in their own back garden, which could also be seen as a form of nest cleaning. Other dogs have a particular fondness for rabbit poo, sheep poo, horse poo or cat poo.

Eating dog poo isn't bad for your dog per se, so long as it's regularly wormed. In fact, the main issue with poo-eating is usually that it tests the relationship between dog and owner; humans find it a repulsive habit. Eating the poo of other animals (and the chances are we won't discriminate) can have other issues – they may contain parasites, viruses, bacteria or traces of medication.

Dachshund Fact

- **Famous film star** dachshund owners have included: John Wayne, Clark Gable, Gary Cooper, Clint Eastwood, Jean Harlow, Marlon Brando, Leonard Nimoy, Carole Lombard, Brigitte Bardot, Audrey Hepburn, Elizabeth Taylor, Doris Day, Paul Newman and Joanne Woodward, Al Pacino, George Harrison, Lou Reed, David Bowie, Jack Black, Kelsey Grammer, Liv Ullmann and Kim Cattrall.

Punishing me won't work, as I simply don't understand what the problem is, and I never will. Dietary additives (such as pineapple) or using unpleasant tasting substances such as chilli or pepper added to my food to flavour my poo are rarely effective either.

First and foremost, pick up all poo as soon as it's deposited – if it's not there I can't eat it. Nor can other dogs.

As with all behavioural issues, the best approach is a reward-based training scheme. You'll need to keep my top favourite treats to hand for this – fish, cheese or sausages will usually suffice – this needs to be a seriously tasty treat to distract me! Either prepare a word that you'll use only in this situation, attract my attention, use the word and throw the food down. Keep your fingers crossed. It might not work initially but keep at it. Little by little I should lose interest and race toward my special treat. This system requires real perseverance on your part. Simultaneously work on reinforcing my 'leave' training.

Giving me a dental chew stick in the garden after a walk should clean my mouth effectively; neither of us want you to shrink away from me when I come up for a pat or doggy kiss!

Grooming

Sausage dogs can be smooth, wire-haired or long-haired, and each type has slightly different grooming requirements. All benefit from additional grooming in spring and autumn when we're shedding more.

Wire-haired dachshunds shed the least hair; under the wiry topcoat is a soft, dense undercoat. A brush every two weeks using a bristle brush will suffice, but don't neglect to work through our undercoat to remove dirt and dead skin. We benefit from a trip to the groomer twice a year.

Smooth-haired dachshunds need a weekly brush; use soft bristle brushes or a grooming mitt. My hair may be short, but I will still shed and will need help maintaining my smooth, glossy coat.

Long-haired dachshunds require the most grooming to remove tangles and dirt from our silky hair. Brush us gently starting with our back, then working down the legs. You may want to section the hair so you can work through it systematically. Pay particular attention to the feet, where our fur matts, and the ears. And don't neglect the tummy. Use a combination of a bristle brush, a slicker brush with rows of fine metal teeth, and a sturdy metal comb with rotating teeth. Please be gentle. It won't

hurt to have a small pair of scissors handy to cut out some stubborn knots.

Frequent grooming will help us to keep ourselves clean and healthy and, if you use the right equipment, we will enjoy the experience. Regular brushing stimulates blood circulation and spreads my natural oils through my coat, which should help ensure I look at my glossiest best. This is also a good opportunity for you to give me the once-over and make sure I'm healthy, with no unexplained lumps and bumps.

Bathing

Sausage dogs tend not to be natural water lovers, which doesn't make bathing the happiest of experiences. If you need to bathe me, wet me thoroughly, avoiding my face and ears, then apply a dog shampoo for sensitive skin. Give me a good rub all over to clean my fur then rinse me gently, making sure you remove all traces of shampoo, any residue will cause irritation. Please avoid getting any water in my ears – it might trigger an ear infection. Clean my face separately with a clean cloth dipped in warm water then wrung out.

Once I'm clean, have lots of warm towels to hand. Put one on the floor, place me onto it then put another towel on top of me. Rub me briskly.

Ears

If you keep my ears clean it will help me to avoid ear infections. Every couple of weeks dip a cotton wool ball in warm water, squeeze it out so it's damp – not dripping – and gently wipe the inside of my ears. Never use a cotton bud on me. Dry my ears gently.

Smile Please

You can help to keep my teeth clean by giving me raw bones to chew, or you can get specially designed chews that are supposed to help prevent the build-up of plaque and tartar. Feeding me with dry food is also helpful.

If I develop bad breath this may indicate gum disease, and a serious build-up of tartar will require the vet to give my teeth a deep clean. This has to be done under anaesthetic, it's an unnecessary expense for you and I certainly won't enjoy the experience. What's more, neglecting my teeth can lead to the development of other serious health problems.

You can also clean my teeth every couple of days. Use special doggy toothpaste that tastes of meat, so I don't mind the experience. Do not use human toothpaste on me, as it can be harmful. Gently rub the toothpaste over my teeth – get me used to this experience by simply rubbing a little bit of doggy toothpaste over a couple of teeth, nothing more. Gradually increase the amounts of toothpaste and time spent on the task over a week or so. Get me used to you manipulating my lips so that you can reach all areas of my teeth, either use a small toothbrush or a finger-brush to clean my teeth. Give me plenty of treats to reward me.

Ask the vet to check my teeth occasionally, perhaps when I go in for my annual inoculation, to make sure no problems are developing.

Pedicure

My nails shouldn't be allowed to get too long. Pavement walking helps to keep them in shape, but you'll still need to trim my nails. Get someone knowledgeable to show you how to do this or leave it to the professionals.

My nail contains the quick; the vessel that brings blood to the nail. If you cut my nail too short you'll cut this, it'll be painful and I will bleed. I will also not want you to come anywhere near my nails again. The fact that my nails are often brown or black, though there are exceptions, makes this task harder as you can't see the quick as easily, so don't feel bad about getting the professionals to do this job for you.

If you can hear my nails click-click-clacking when I walk across a hard floor it's a sign that my nails are too long. Uncut nails can lead to lameness.

A little and often is the best policy for pedicures. If you trim my nails every two weeks, you'll only need to take off a small piece of the nail. I will be suspicious of this process initially but in time I will relax and behave while you give me my pedicure.

When you are giving me a pedicure and have hold of my paw, take the opportunity to examine my pads and toes to make sure everything is in good shape.

Tiny Companions

All animals accommodate a host of tiny friends, and us dachshunds are no exception. Whether I'm smooth, long-haired or wire-haired, there are still plenty of places for all kinds of things to hide.

Fleas

As sure as night follows day I will get fleas. Fleas are everywhere; cats and humans shouldn't get too high and mighty about them, because you have your own cat fleas and human fleas too. I can pick them up from another dog, a cat, your home, your friend's home or from your clothes or your shoes.

These tiny parasites are superb jumpers, which is how they hop from their environment, to host, to home, to host and so on. Females must have a meal of blood before they lay eggs; up to 50 eggs per day. The eggs are like tiny grains of sand, and they fall off me when they are laid, then hatch into larvae within two to five days. The larvae are around 5mm (1/4in) long and live in carpets, soft furnishings and cracks in the floorboards. They feed and after around two weeks build a cocoon, from which they pupate as adult fleas when a food source is nearby. The entire life cycle takes

around three to four weeks. Fleas can also pass tapeworm on to me.

Fleas are particularly active when the weather is warmer, but they can still reproduce inside the home in winter. Moreover, fleas can lie dormant in a home for a long time when there's no food source, but the arrival of a pet stimulates them to hatch. If you are moving house, make sure my flea treatments are up to date.

Dog fleas prefer dogs and cat fleas prefer cats, but they will hop onto any host under extreme circumstances – even you! If you are getting bitten by fleas it suggests that our home has a serious flea problem.

If I have fleas, bear in mind that only approximately 5 per cent of the flea population will be on me, and the remaining 95 per cent will be in our home! Spot on treatments, which are effective, only kill the adult fleas, so if there's an infestation it can take up to three months to eradicate the problem. The best solution is to consistently use appropriate preventative flea treatments from the moment I come into your life as a puppy.

Puppies require specific flea treatments suitable for their age and weight; the earliest they can be administered is usually at eight weeks old. Some treatments aren't suitable for young puppies, so you should always consult your vet for advice. Fleas can trouble puppies badly. They can have an adverse reaction to flea bites, leading to allergic dermatitis, and in severe infestations a puppy can develop life-threatening anaemia.

How can you tell if I have fleas? Scratching is a tell-tale sign, but you can see evidence of fleas too; part my coat at the back of my neck, or near my ears, or at the base of my tail and look for tiny black specks that look like pepper. This is flea dirt, basically digested blood and unsavoury. If you put this on a piece of paper and dampen it, it will turn red and you have your proof that I have fleas.

Chemical spot-on treatments, administered to the back of the neck and between the shoulder blades, are effective. These will also render all the flea eggs infertile. Live fleas will be killed within 24 hours and some flea treatments also kill ticks.

Please remember to wash my pet bedding regularly, hoover floors thoroughly and don't forget the soft furnishings. Empty the contents of the dust bag after hoovering!

If you follow this regime fleas should never become a problem. However, if you do let things slide and your house has a serious flea infestation – you'll probably be being bitten too at this point – you'll also need to use a chemical spray treatment on your house to help kill the pesky things.

If you want to use 'natural' herbal preparations, please check with your vet first. The ingredients in some products are, ironically, not safe for use around dogs or cats. Cat flea treatments aren't safe for use on dogs either, and vice versa!

Ticks

Like fleas, ticks will climb onto me when I'm out on a walk, then enjoy a drink of my blood. The tick will stay in place until it has had enough to drink, after which it will drop off. Ticks can cause severe skin irritation and can also transmit Lyme disease, *Borreliosis*, a tick-transmitted

bacterial infection found in Europe, North America and Asia that can affect humans and dogs.

Ticks are found in areas where there's wildlife or livestock and are most commonly seen in warmer weather. They start off small, but grow as they feed – you can see these or feel them on me, my short coat usually ensures they are spotted quickly.

Ticks resemble a skin tag and can be light in colour, grey or dark. The part you can see is the tick's large, flat body (if you look closely you can see its legs). Don't attempt to pull it straight off me – this can result in cross-contamination as parts of the mouth can remain in place.

Ticks are easily removed with a tick tool that allows you to anchor the body while you then twist the tool. This unscrews the tick from its food source. Once you have removed the tick, squash it between some paper and dispose of the body. It's best to purchase a tick tool when you get a puppy – they're cheap to buy and available from most pet shops. Vaccinations against Lyme disease are now available if you are concerned that I'm at high risk.

Margot

Owned by Amelia | Lives in Dorset, England | @margotdapple

Margot loves nothing more than playing outside
with other dogs, then coming home for a cuddle
and nap. Her favourite toys are her Nemo
clownfish and anything that squeaks!

If you are worried that your dachshund may have contracted Lyme disease from a tick, take it to the vet.

Worms

Dogs can pick up worms from numerous sources; soil, vegetation or faeces can be contaminated with worm eggs and contaminated fleas can pass tapeworm to your dog. Worms can be passed from dog to dog via their faeces and, though it's unusual, it can also be passed on to you. It's another good reason for all dog owners to scoop that poop!

Worms can cause diarrhoea and vomiting, weight loss, weakness, coughing and anaemia. Puppies with worms get an abnormally swollen tummy. If you see me scooting – dragging my bottom along the floor – it's an indication that I might have worms,

though I can do this for other reasons too, so get me checked out by the vet.

Intestinal Worms

Roundworms are passed on to a puppy via its mother's milk, and adult dogs can contract them from contaminated soil or meat. These look like wriggling bits of spaghetti in your dog's poo!

Hookworms and whipworms live in my intestines where they latch on with sharp teeth to suck my blood. Weight loss is a common symptom and I contract them via contaminated soil.

Tapeworms are spread by infected fleas. They can also be spotted around my anus and look like grains of rice in my poo – they're actually small segments of the tapeworm. I pick them up if I accidentally ingest an infected flea while grooming myself. As the flea is digested the tapeworm egg is released and hatches, whereupon it latches on to my small intestine. Occasionally an entire tapeworm can be passed or vomited up – not a pleasant experience for anyone, so keep on top of my flea control!

Symptoms include:
- Fever
- Lethargy
- Limping
- Swollen lymph nodes

All dogs should be regularly wormed, and there are numerous deworming medications available. Puppies are at particular risk from worms but please seek advice from your vet before worming your puppy.

Lungworm

Lungworm (*Angiostrongylus vasorum*) is common in some countries and it can kill. I can contract it if I consume its larvae, which is found in infected slugs, snails and frogs. Dogs can accidentally eat small slugs if they are on their toys or their fur. The lungworm moves through the dog's body and finally settles in the heart and blood vessels. We excrete the larvae in our poo – this infects more slugs and snails, which can then infect more dogs.

Symptoms include:
- Coughing
- Breathing problems
- Reluctance to exercise
- Abnormal blood clotting

Take your dog to the vet to be checked out if they are displaying any of these symptoms. The vet will need to prescribe a special course of medication to eliminate lungworm. In some areas where lungworm is especially prevalent it's advisable to give your dog preventative medication.

Heartworm

Dirofilariasis is transmitted via the bite of an infected mosquito and affects dogs, cats and ferrets. It's found in large swathes of the USA and Canada but is rarely seen in the UK. There are 30 species of mosquito that transmit it. Heartworm kills dogs, but as it takes several years before symptoms appear, the disease is often well advanced by the time clinical signs are visible. Blood tests can confirm a diagnosis and X-rays will show the extent of the damage. Medication is given via a series of injections. It's critical that dogs are kept quiet during treatment and for several months afterwards, never easy for a dachshund. If you live in areas where heartworm can be contracted preventive medication is recommended.

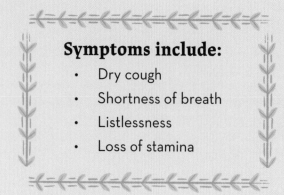

Symptoms include:

- Dry cough
- Shortness of breath
- Listlessness
- Loss of stamina

Mites

Ear mites (*Otodectes cynotis*) are common in cats, but can affect dogs as well, so if your dog has ear mites, always check their feline friends too. The parasites live in the outer ear canal. Symptoms included ear scratching and shaking of the head so that the ears flap. The ear will become red and inflamed and you may see a waxy brown discharge. Untreated ear mites can lead to other ear infections. The ear will need to be regularly cleaned and treated with medicated ear drops prescribed by the vet. Regular flea treatment should act as a preventative.

Fur mites (*Cheyletiellosis*) known as 'walking dandruff', is a common canine mite. This small, white mite lives on the surface of the skin and causes mild itchiness – one of the obvious signs of an infestation is a coat full of small flakes of skin, or scurf.

The harvest mite (*Neotrombicula autumnalis*) is a small, bright orange mite that can also affect cats and humans. It can easily be picked up in grassy areas or woodland in late summer and autumn. This mite causes intense itching and inflammation in the feet and lower leg, as well as scabs and pus, but it can also affect the armpits, the tummy and the genitals, and occasionally the ears. It can be seen with the naked eye, and is easily treated with an insecticide. Anti-inflammatories may be required to ease discomfort. Regular flea treatments should deal with this problem without it ever becoming an issue.

Mange

There are two types of skin mites that can cause mange: *Demodex canis*, and *Sarcoptes scabiei*. A dog with a good immune system should not fall prey to demodectic mange, but puppies can be at risk as they cannot stop the parasite and it's usually passed from mother to pup. The parasite lives within hair follicles and causes the skin to become itchy; hair loss and lesions can develop. It spreads from the point of infection and across the whole body – the dog's skin appears to turn a blue/grey. You won't be able to see these parasites with the naked eye, they can only be seen through a microscope. This form of mange doesn't easily spread to other dogs or to humans, and is treated with a topical preparation.

Scabies, however, is highly contagious. I don't have to come into direct contact with another creature to catch it. All dogs in the household will need to be treated with a medicated shampoo. This is a zoonotic disease, which means it can be passed on to humans. Foxes are common source of contagion.

Health and First Aid

As you well know, I love my food, but indulging me isn't a kindness. Obesity is one of the biggest threats to the health of a dachshund. Slipping us illicit treats from your plate may feel like an expression of love, but our long back is easily damaged and carrying extra weight stresses it still further. As a breed we're also susceptible to diabetes and obesity is a trigger. If you use treats for training purposes only and give me sufficient exercise (an hour a day) you should have a happy, healthy dachshund.

Even with our muscular physique, every dachshund can suffer from the cold. Our wet and muddy, low-lying bodies need protection in winter when temperatures plummet. If neglected, we can suffer from hypothermia. Depending on your local temperatures I may need a fleece or a waterproof padded jacket to stop my temperature dropping too low. Plus, as I hate the rain, a waterproof coat can help me cope with the wet.

The Kennel Club in the UK has a programme called Breed Watch that is designed to serve as an early warning system for points of concern in dog breeds. There are three categories:

Category 1 is breeds with no current points of concern; Category 2 highlights breed points of concern; Category 3 identifies breeds that have visible conditions or exaggerations that can cause pain or discomfort. All varieties of dachshund are classified as Category 2 with the following points of concern:

- Significantly underweight
- Sore eyes or excessive tearing
- Incorrect hindquarter movement or unsound movement

Pills and Medicine

Please don't give me any form of human medicine unless my vet specifically suggests it and advises the dosage.

Prescribed liquid medication is easy to administer if you have a little doggy medicine syringe – nine times out of ten this comes with the medicine. The dose will be specified and marked on the syringe. Fill up the syringe to the required mark, then pop it into the side of my mouth, pointing the syringe toward my throat and squeezing quickly. This is usually a straightforward operation.

Pills can be more of a challenge. You can try holding my body gently between your legs, get the pill in one hand and with the other lift my head upwards and open my mouth. You want to drop the pill towards the back of my throat. Hold my jaw closed and stroke my throat to encourage me to swallow.

This may be easier with me than other dog breeds because of my enthusiasm to eat anything and everything. Some pills come in dog-friendly flavours, so if you act like you are giving me a great treat I may be convinced, but if I'm not fooled try one of the following techniques.

If I generally have dry food, you can try popping the pill into some wet food and giving me that to eat. Alternatively, utilize something slightly moist, such as cream cheese or pâté to sweeten the pill. Pop the pill inside a little ball of something delicious, again act like you are giving me a treat, get me to sit and offer the camouflaged pill – the chances are we will wolf it down. Processed human foods aren't good for us, but in extremis, small amounts can be utilized.

First aid kit

For when accidents occur, it's helpful to have a first aid kit to hand, which should include:

- Antiseptic wipes
- Pressurized saline wound wash
- Dog antiseptic cream
- Sterile gauze dressings
- Self-adhesive bandage
- A dog boot, in case of cut or injured paws

Cuts

Sausage dogs are small but fearless. Flying along that close to the ground leaves me vulnerable to injuries - a stray bramble can cause a lot of damage. If I injure myself, it may look worse than it is. If I've been running my heart will be beating fast, and I will be pumping blood out of my cut with some velocity. The first thing to do is to get me to sit down to slow my heartbeat. This will allow you to assess the severity of the injury. Apply gentle pressure to the cut.

If you are unsure, please contact my vet straight away for advice and don't let me do anything active until I've been checked out. If stitches are required, the sooner it's done the better, although I will be ungrateful and won't thank you. The vet will have to anaesthetize me and may need to keep me in overnight. I will be wobbly after an anaesthetic, so please carry me into the house. Help me onto my bed or onto the sofa so I can be close to you. I will sleep.

I will also need the 'cone of shame' (buster collar), or a medical pet shirt, because I will not leave stitches or dressings alone, though I don't understand why not. These specially designed devices prevent me from doing any damage to myself. Leave it on at night to be on the safe side or you'll wake to find I've removed my dressing and all of my stitches which will require another trip to the vet - costly for you and traumatic for me. Be firm.

The collar can come off on walks and for meals - I will be able to access my water bowl with it on no matter what I would have you believe. Medical vests come off for walks and toilet breaks.

If my foot has been injured you may have to cover it with some kind of plastic shoe so that the dressing doesn't get wet – even in summer, the grass can be covered with dew in the morning.

I will be on lead walks for a minimum of ten days – the vet will guide you. They will want to give me regular check-ups to ensure that everything is healing as it should, and any dressings will need to be regularly changed. Even if I seem to be healing nicely, don't let me off the lead until the vet gives you the all-clear. I can rip stitches open if I'm allowed to run free.

Heat Exhaustion

All dog owners should be aware not to leave us in cars in full sun or even in the shade when it's hot. To keep us safe, it's best not to leave us in the car alone at all, not ever! Even five minutes can be too long, because as you humans know, shops can have queues, or you bump into someone you know, and before you know it half an hour has passed and I'm dying of the heat.

By the same token you should be careful when you travel with me on long journeys. Give me frequent breaks, the chance to stretch my legs, relieve myself, have a drink and get some shade.

If I'm panting rapidly, making an unusual sound, starting to produce foamy saliva, vomiting or if my tongue is red and floppy and I seem disorientated, confused or start swaying, I've dangerously overheated.

The first thing to do is to cool me down. Putting a hose on me or plunging me into cold water will be too much of a shock. Instead, wet a large towel with cool (not cold) water and place it over me. Put a fan on me or gently sprinkle water over the towel every so often – a watering can with a sprinkler head on will do the trick. Overheating to this extent can cause long term damage and I should be checked out by the vet. It can take me some days to recover from heat exhaustion.

This is a shocking experience for me and for you, so please don't let me run around on a hot day. Exercise me first thing in the morning, or late in the evening when it's cooler. Keep me indoors in the shade where I can stay cool.

Diarrhoea

If the world is falling out of my bottom, the chances are that either you have made a dramatic alteration to my diet, which may not suit me, or (more likely) I've scavenged something to eat that has not agreed with me. As already stated, we sausage dogs are greedy and like nothing better than chomping on something illicit we find on a walk.

The first course of action is to withhold food for a day, but please make sure I've water on hand, as diarrhoea can lead to dehydration. After 24 hours feed me something bland (but appreciated!); cooked chicken or white fish with boiled rice is ideal. Just give me a small portion and allow me plenty of time to digest it before giving me a little bit more. This will usually sort everything out and I can return to normal feeding. However, if things don't improve please take me to the vet.

If you see blood in my faeces, or if am vomiting, contact the vet straight away.

Vomiting

I will vomit sometimes, all dogs do. Sometimes it may be that I've gobbled my food too quickly. If this happens you'll probably be horrified to see me happily tucking in to eat the whole splatted mess. Greedy puppies are especially prone to this, so if it happens regularly, feed me the same amount but split it into smaller portions to eat throughout the day and use a slow feeding bowl. Don't let me tear around straight after eating.

I like to eat grass, but I may vomit after eating it, but don't worry about this.

If I vomit repeatedly, I may have eaten something unpleasant. Follow the same principle of withholding food for 24 hours then feeding a bland diet, as with diarrhoea above.

If I'm vomiting frequently, or if you notice something resembling blood, or faecal matter – that smells foul – take me straight to the vet.

Coughing

An occasional cough is nothing to worry about, but a regular cough should be checked out by my vet.

Kennel cough is an airborne disease, usually a virus, that easily spreads between dogs. I can be inoculated

annually against kennel cough and the vaccination will reduce my chances of catching it and reduce my symptoms if I do. Most boarding kennels insist that I'm inoculated against kennel cough before a stay. If I am not vaccinated, I can pick up kennel cough from infected dogs. Most dogs with kennel cough aren't too poorly, but some of us can be badly affected and may need anti-inflammatories to bring down our temperature and reduce inflammation in our airways. If I'm lethargic, refusing to eat or developing breathing problems, take me straight to the vet.

You'll need to keep me away from other dogs for two to three weeks after my symptoms have disappeared. Don't let me race around if I have kennel cough as this can make symptoms worse. Instead, give me gentle exercise on a lead.

A cough can also be indicative of heart disease, especially if it happens after exercise or in the evening. Get me checked out by a vet who will listen to my heart to make sure that this isn't the cause of the coughing.

Ears

My distinctive ears fall forwards and the front edges brush against my check. The good news is that dachshunds aren't particularly prone to ear problems, though the long-haired breeds may be more susceptible. Keep my ears clean and check them regularly (see the grooming chapter).

If my ears are red, hot to the touch and itchy – I keep rubbing them with my paws or on the carpet – and have an unpleasant smell, I might have an ear infection. Please take me to see the vet as I might need drops, ointment or antibiotics.

If I start scratching my ear or shaking my head, have a look inside – there may be a grass seed, a burr or some other foreign body that is causing discomfort. If you can see something obvious,

Dachshund Fact

- The miniature dachshund is the smallest member of the hound group.

remove it gently – damp cotton wool is good for this. Don't probe into the ear or use ear buds. If the foreign body doesn't lift out easily, I will need a trip to the vet.

If you can see a dark discharge in the ear that looks like coffee grounds, I may have ear mites (see the tiny companions chapter). If my ear is red, I may have an infection – once again a trip to the vet is in order. Over-the-counter products aren't recommended, instead consult an expert.

Skin Irritation

Skin allergies can have a number of trigger factors. Oversensitivity can be caused by fleas (see the tiny companions chapter), pollen, grass, moulds, house-dust mites and some foods. The skin becomes itchy, red and can be hot to the touch. Bald patches and skin infections can develop. It's essential you practise a through and regular grooming regime, please see the chapter on grooming. Please make an appointment for me to see the vet if you are concerned, skin problems tend to get worse if they are left untreated,

they will help you to determine what are my trigger factors (see the diet chapter).

Bites

If you own a dog, the chances are that at some point they will become involved in some nose-to-nose power posturing. We sausage dogs can act provocatively, being vocal, snarling and suspicious of larger dogs. If we decide to engage in a set-to, we're likely to come off worst. If we get bitten have us checked out – we may need a shot of antibiotics to make sure the wound doesn't get infected.

Wasps and Bees

Just like humans, we will suffer irritation if we're stung by wasps and bees. First, check to make sure that the sting itself isn't still stuck in me. If it is, remove it carefully, scraping it out rather than pulling it out as this can release more venom. Bathe the area with cool water to help reduce the swelling. Most dogs suffer minor pain and irritation, however if the area is swelling rapidly or if the dog is having difficulty breathing or vomiting, take it straight to the emergency vet.

Frankie

Owned by Nikala | Lives in Edinburgh, Scotland | @frankietheminidaxie

Frankie is a super laid back, confident and
friendly dachshund who loves to explore the
local beaches and woodlands. She also enjoys a
good nap and being the centre of attention.

Snake Bites

Snake bites can be fatal. In the UK it's only the adder that can cause us serious harm, but in countries such as America and Australia, there are far more venomous snakes that can strike. If you see your dachshund worrying something in the grass, call them to you immediately.

Most snake bites occur in the spring and summer months. If you think your dachshund has been bitten, keep them quiet and calm and take them to the vet as a matter of urgency. If you see the snake attack, make a note of its markings as this will help the vet administer the correct anti-venom. You can tie a constricting band above the bite to slow the spread of the venom. This should be snug but not too tight.

Symptoms to look out for include:

- A small wound with fang marks
- Swelling of the affected area
- Collapse (though they can recover temporarily)
- Sudden weakness
- Vomiting
- Hypersalivation
- Dilated pupils
- Twitching of the muscles

Fireworks

Like all other dogs, we hate fireworks – once we become sensitized to the noise we will always be frightened. Prevention is the best cure; don't ever take me to a firework display and don't let me be outside if you hear fireworks being let off nearby. If I wasn't frightened by fireworks before, I will become hyper-sensitive to them if I'm near some that are being set off.

The best thing is to avoid creating a phobia in the first place. If you know fireworks are going to be let off in the vicinity of your home, keep me indoors. Take me for a good walk before it gets dark, so that I won't need toilet breaks during the evening. Turn up the volume on the television or the radio to drown out the noise and don't leave me home alone. Stay calm and ignore any bangs to give me the message that this isn't something I need to worry about.

You can try de-sensitizing therapies to gradually get me accustomed to strange noises. Suitable sounds can be downloaded online and you can play them to me, carefully controlling the volume, starting quietly. This is a slow process and I should not be alarmed at any stage, but get gently acclimatized to hearing the sounds, while you play with me and feed me with this quiet noise in the background. Over the weeks, you can raise the volume and I will learn that this isn't a threatening sound.

If my phobia is severe the vet can recommend some natural therapies and possibly pheromone treatments to make me feel more secure. Tranquillizers are a last resort, but these won't cure the terror, just make us sleepy.

Genetic issues

Intervertebral Disk Disease (IVDD)
The dachshunds' long spine makes us susceptible to back problems. The vertebrae in our back and neck are cushioned one from the other by intervertebral discs. If these discs degenerate, they can shift position resulting in a slipped or ruptured disc. This can happen gradually or can be the result of a jump from a piece of furniture. It's painful, and the dog's movement will be impaired – they can be paralyzed, and their bowel and bladder affected. Please see a vet as a matter of urgency if you think there are problems. Treatment may require confining the dog in a small space for up to six weeks with short lead walks permitted and treating them with anti-inflammatories to reduce swelling. Surgery can be successful if undertaken promptly.

Hip and Elbow Dysplasia
This is caused when the hip or elbow ball and socket is poorly developed and the joint becomes unstable. Signs of dysplasia usually show between the ages of five to 18 months of age.

Instances of hip dysplasia are decreasing. However, even with parental checks, genetics can play a part and dysplasia can still be a problem for sausage dogs. Treatment is mostly directed towards preventing further deterioration, reducing inflammation and easing pain. Weight loss can help if obesity is an issue, and rest and controlled exercise are beneficial. Physiotherapy may be recommended. Surgery can be an option in some cases.

Symptoms include:
- Limping and lameness
- Difficulty getting up
- Difficulty walking uphill
- Waddling walk
- Reluctance to exercise or climb stairs

Luxating Patella

This occurs when the kneecap – the patella – slips out of place and moves to one side or the other. It causes considerable pain and should be dealt with promptly so that the condition cannot further deteriorate and lead to arthritis. Unfortunately, sausage dogs are susceptible to this genetic condition,

and weight gain can aggravate it. Signs to look out for are lameness, obvious pain, an occasional skipping gait and stiffness in the affected limb – it can be seen in puppies. If you see this take us to the vet straight away and inform your breeder.

Pes Varus

This is a genetic bone deformity where the legs acquire a bow-legged look with the feet turning inwards, and causes lameness. It occurs when the growth plates on the outside of the shinbone grow faster than those on the inside, and becomes noticeable when puppies are six to eight months old. Surgery can help, and the earlier it's done the better the prognosis. This is a condition that must be managed and carefully monitored. It more commonly affects miniature dachshunds.

Lafora Disease

This is an inherited type of epilepsy caused by a faulty gene that miniature wire-haired dachshunds can be affected by. Genetic screening has helped reduce the prevalence and all reputable

breeders should provide Lafora screening certificates.

Cushing's Syndrome

Cushing's occurs when the body's adrenal gland overproduces the cortisol steroid hormone and weakens the immune system. The usual cause is a tumour on the adrenal or pituitary gland. Symptoms include excessive thirst and urination, panting, weight gain, swelling around the belly and fatigue. This condition cannot be cured, but it can be successfully managed.

Progressive Retinal Atrophy (PRA), Cataracts and Glaucoma

Dachshunds are prone to some eye problems – the miniature breeds more so. If you see any issues with eyesight, if I start rubbing my eyes excessively, start bumping into things or seeming more unsure in the dark, consult the vet. Dachshunds are prone to dry eyes, cataracts and, if they gain weight, glaucoma. Tests can determine whether dogs carry PRA – a mutated gene that can lead to a gradual loss of sight

over months or years and, at worst, to blindness. There's no cure for this disease, so DNA testing is the best hope for gradual eradication. If your dog seems to be unsure in the dark or starts bumping into things, take them to the vet to be checked. Also, being so close to the ground means dachshunds' eyes are more vulnerable to injury, and a scratch in the eye can lead to corneal ulcers – always consult a vet.

Dachshund Fact

- The German royal family were ardent dachshund fanciers. Kaiser Wilhelm II had a ferocious pair called Wadl and Hexl who famously caught and killed one of Archduke Franz Ferdinand's famous and prized golden pheasants on a visit to his country château in 1914.

Index

Further Reading

Anderson, David, *The Complete Guide to Miniature Dachshunds*, Amazon, 2018

Hoppendale, George and Asia Moore, *Dachshund*, IMB Publishing, 2015

Moore, Asia, *The Complete Happy Dachshund Guide*, Worldwide Information
   Publishing, 2020

Richie, Vanessa, *The Complete Guide to Dachshunds*, LP Media Inc., 2020

Seymour, Alex, *Miniature and Standard Dachshunds*, CWP Publishing, 2016

Whitwam, Linda, *The Dachshund Handbook*, Canine Handbooks, 2020

Acknowledgements

My thanks must go to Jimmy the Lurcher, our first family dog, who turned this cat-loving, dog-hating mother of two into an ardent dog-worshipper. We grew up together and he seduced me, batting his long blonde eyelashes and generally behaving abominably. Jimmy was a living, breathing incarnation of a badly-behaved dog and together we discovered how dog training can transform your life.

Every dog owner will get to know numerous dachshunds as they walk their dogs, for they have great personalities. I must thank Val Hennessey for giving me the chance to get to know her dachshund, Gertie. She and my lurcher Jimmy conducted a passionate love affair, though two less obviously compatible companions it would be hard to find. Val trusted me with dog-sitting duties and Gertie inducted me in the charms of sausage dogs. I must also thank James Knowles and his three gorgeous dachshunds, Masha, Winnie and Fanta, who patiently answered my many questions and further sold me to the charms of the dachshund.

I must also thank the many nameless dachshund owners who tolerated queries from a complete stranger, and who allowed me to pet their pooches. I've yet to meet a dachshund owner who would contemplate owning any other breed of dog.

I must thank my husband Eric, without whose patient nagging I would never have discovered that dog-owning was a good thing. For this and all kinds of other things, I owe him a huge debt of gratitude. Our children, Florence and Teddy, have patiently endured their parents' dog-worshipping tendencies and embraced the delights of dog walking in the rain. They are the first to point out if the house ever smells of dog, so keep me on my domestic toes, and are quick to highlight any pungent emissions of canine wind. Florence also proofread an early draft of this book.

At Batsford I must, as always, thank Polly Powell for her faith in me. Lilly Phelan has been the kindest and gentlest of editors and a delight to work with and Gemma Doyle must be thanked for her superb design.